Watch What You Say When You Talk To Yourself

Vitaminds to Ponder

by

Dr. Bob Gerding

authorHOUSE™

1663 LIBERTY DRIVE, SUITE 200
BLOOMINGTON, INDIANA 47403
(800) 839-8640
WWW.AUTHORHOUSE.COM

First published by AuthorHouse 03/14/05

ISBN: 1-4208-3280-8 (sc)

Printed in the United States of America
Bloomington, Indiana

This book is printed on acid-free paper.

Dedication

This book, "Watch what you say when you talk to yourself", is thoughtfully and lovingly dedicated to my two children, Bethany and Brian. They have been the apple of my eye since the day of their birth. It is my hope that they will accept this manuscript as a gift both now and for many years to come.

As I have grown with them in my life, they have been a great inspiration to me. They have given me much more joy and happiness than I could ever repay. And for that, I want to say to both of them, "Thank you." Just remember to watch what you say when you talk to yourself.

Love Dad,

Dr. Bob Gerding

Table of Contents

Attitude

We must understand that the most dangerous disease of all is the hardening of the attitudes. At last count, there were over 600 schools per state on average in America. These schools teach everything from pig farming , cosmetology, ballet dancing, boxing, trimming toenails, heart surgery, software development, hardware repair, subtraction to addition, division to multiplication, Cooking, counseling, preaching, teaching, and a host of other topics and subjects.

Yet, they all agree. No matter if, you are a doctor, lawyer, teacher, preacher, office worker, line worker or politician; you share the precise same judgment. Your attitude as you carry out a project is the central factor in its success and achievement.

Without a doubt, we know that your attitude is more important than your aptitude. Give me a person with a great attitude and you can help him acquire the aptitude. Yet, sad to say, we have so many people that have exalted aptitude at the cost of attitude.

This is not something schools teach, nor can they. Attitude is caught, not taught. You catch it as you grow and get an understanding of the "big" picture in life. You catch it as you are around those that have learned that life is about attitude.

You can change your life and the outlook you have about it, by changing your attitude.

However, what is attitude? Let us consider the following idea.

Can you still hear those words as they bounce around in your memory? "You better change your attitude or else." On the other hand, how about this one, "That attitude of yours is going to get you in trouble one of these days." Finally, remember this, "As far as I am concerned, a good attitude adjustment would do you good." Or, "Thank you for having such a good attitude about the situation."

Attitude is the management of one's affairs; the reaction to an action; It is the state of mind or feelings concerning some matter; A mental or moral disposition; It is the way you react or respond to the affairs of life.

Now let us illustrate this from a book that reveals a lot about the attitudes of human nature, the Bible.

First, look at Cain as he responds about the whereabouts of his slain brother Abel. (See Genesis chapter 4) Cain's answer was "Am I my brother's keeper?" This attitude reveals that Cain was saying he did not have time to watch over his brother Abel and be concerned about where he was.

The Bible is a book that reveals the attitude of many people, and how they responded to life.

We read about the twelve spies in Numbers chapter 13 and 14. Ten of the spies had a rotten attitude and two of the spies had an attitude that said, "Hey folks, we can't lose, God is on our side."

This leads me to the analogy of the thermostat and the

 thermometer. We are like one or the other. The thermometer is regulated by an outside influence. The thermometer is always controlled and influenced by its surroundings. Let me illustrate. The thermometer type person is up, if the sun is. They are having a good day, so long as the circumstances are "just right." However, if the clouds are overhead and it looks like rain, the same day (just without the sun) is gloom and doom. These people are controlled by the circumstances and conditions. Remember, we said earlier that the most dangerous disease of all is the hardening of the attitude.

On the other hand, if it rains, there are those that have good reason to enjoy the day anyway. These are the Thermostat type people. They are in control in how they react to the circumstances and conditions of life. These people realize that each day is a miniature lifetime, so they decide to enjoy it to the fullest. Each moment of life is a gift. Every now will eventually accumulate into a completed day. Eventually, every completed day accumulates into a lifetime, but it all has its nucleus in now. How is your attitude now?

Let us further illustrate this by the rhyme that says, "Two men looked out of prison bars, one saw mud, the other, stars." The outlook was different for both people in the same condition. One looked up the other looked down. Which direction are you looking today?

Why is attitude so important? Have you ever read a birth announcement declaring that the new born was a famous teacher, singer, writer, preacher, worker or some other job title or designation, of course not.

We must understand that the real rewards in life are due more to your behavior (Attitude) than your birth.

Therefore, we must learn to do away with garbage dump thinking.

Suppose I came to your house with several sacks of gross, smelly, stinky trash and dumped them smack dab in the middle of your living room floor. I then demanded that you had to put up with it. In addition, suppose I suggested that this is the way your living room floor should look. After all other people have the same "look" and "smell."

Now, would you say this sort of thing would be bizarre? Yet, how many of us permit ourselves to allow our minds to be "dumped" on every day. Someone else tries to help us to decide how we ought to respond to a given situation. Therefore, they take the liberty to dump into our minds. Moreover, before you know it, we are on the same defeated path that so many others have taken. We end up with stinking thinking. Do not allow others (or yourself) to use your mind as a garbage dump. No matter what title they wear on their shirt or letterhead.

You can literally alter your life by altering your attitude. Yet, you must be careful about altering your attitude and make sure that you change it according to the right set of standards.

In Romans chapter 12, verse 1 and 2 we read the following words, Romans 12:1-2- "I beseech you therefore, brethren, by the mercies of God, that ye present your bodies a living sacrifice, holy, acceptable unto God, which is your reasonable service. And be not conformed to this world: but be ye transformed by the renewing of your mind, that ye may prove what is that good, and acceptable, and perfect, will of God." We must seek to renew our mind by way of the Scriptures and the counsel that it gives. Remember, we move in the direction of our current dominant thought. Make it a lifestyle to first look into the scripture to understand the correct response to a given situation. Your thinking has a bearing on the way you respond. So be careful what you

Dr. Bob Gerding

allow into your mind. Watch what you dwell upon, and keep your imagination under control. With that said, also feel free to examine that which you hear. Do not take everything that you hear as "gospel." Learn to think on your own two feet. No matter if it is a sermon, songs, or a traditional saying, at all times, learn to examine the words that are bombarding you.

Finally, each day is a miniature lifetime so spend it as if it were the last day of your life. Learn to "relish the moment" it is the only one you have. Having the right attitude will help you with your altitude in life. Learn to live now.

Attitude-Write your thoughts

_____

_____

_____

_____

_____

_____

_____

_____

_____

_____

_____

_____

_____

_____

_____

Break a Vase
(Thoughts on Extravagance)

"Do not touch." "Do not handle." "Stay behind the rope at all times." "Keep your hands off." "If you break it, you buy it."

These are words that we either all have heard or have said ourselves. Such remarks are made about a memorial or things of extravagance. You may say to your child, "Keep your hands off. Do not touch anything in the antique shop. Keep your hands and arms at your side at all times." We say such things because we are looking at articles of rarity and value. We are viewing things of extravagance.

The word extravagance means to go beyond reasonable or moderate limits. It carries with it the thought of luxury and lavishness.

In the Bible, we read a story in Mark chapter fourteen and verses one to nine, (Mk.14:1-9) about a woman which took an alabaster box of ointment of spikenard, (very precious) broke the jar and poured the ointment upon the head of Jesus.

An alabaster box was a reddish marble jar or vase that had been hand carved. It was made of a porous material that would allow the fragrance to slowly escape out of the vase and touch every part of the room. Therefore, the structure of the vase would not allow the ointment to dissipate too quickly. After all, the ointment was very costly and they wanted it to last as long as possible.

We see in the Bible that the woman broke the vase (perhaps the neck of the jar) and poured the costly ointment on Jesus. This act in and of itself was a rare ritual reserved only for royalty. It is said in John chapter twelve and verse three, (Jn.12:3) that the fragrance filled the room. Wherever Jesus went from this point on, the fragrance of the costly spikenard went with him.

Smell the fragrance as Jesus sat in the Passover meal. Then, He went on to the garden to Gethsemane to pray. Afterwards it was off to Herod's judgment hall and finally to the cross. Yet, through the whole event of the anointing, there were some that remained indignant. They were displeased, greatly afflicted and displayed expressions of anger against the woman for what she had done.

This act of anointing looked to be a waste on a peculiar gesture of devotion that paid no dividends. Their only answers were in the words, "It might have been sold." We learn from this that they used the measurement of the world market. They weighed this occasion and life on the stockbrokers scale, the pence.

What then is the lesson for us? In part, we need our hearts and minds shaken out of our arithmetic mode and into love. Put the calculator down and allow an unconditional heart of love to break a vase.

How can we break a vase for someone today? How can we cause a sweet fragrance to be upon a loved one? Remember these words in Matthew chapter twenty-five and verse forty, (Mt.25:40) "If you have done it unto the least of these my brethren, you have done it unto me." You can break a vase by doing something special for another person. Why do we insist on living in a "black and white" world with very little color? Is it because "black and white" is cheaper? We so often conduct our lives according to the lowest bid. Why do we wait until a loved one or friend has been stricken with a tragedy before we are willing to break a vase for them. I think you know the real reason. It is this thing we call pride. We need to get better at swallowing our pride. After all, it is non-fattening and has no carbs?

Do we always need to confine ourselves to the mediocre, the ordinary, or the standard? Perhaps it is time for us to think of someone and break a vase for such a one. Go the extra mile; get off the beaten path of mediocrity and normality. Anyone can follow the norm, so dare to be different.

Go ahead, break a vase for your husband, wife, son, daughter, friend, co-worker, or even for yourself. Put the eyedropper up and get a bucket so you can pour out some extra for that special person. Stop allowing practicality a chance to win over beauty. After all, we use streets of asphalt and concrete. However, in heaven, we see the beauty in the streets of gold. It seems that asphalt and concrete would do. No, Heaven is a place of beauty. Realize that beauty reveals that extra touch and effort as it goes beyond "just getting by." Beauty rises above the level of duty and mediocrity and shows our devotion. Go ahead; lift the dutiful up to the beautiful.

Now, let me be perfectly clear to say that breaking a vase may be different for you than someone else. To one person, breaking a vase could be getting their children a large ice cream cone when a small one would do. (Funds could be a little tight.) On the other hand, to another, breaking a vase could mean going out and buying that special person a diamond ring or a nice watch. It could even be taking the time to write a note of thanks and appreciation to someone. On the other hand, it may be making a phone call to cheer someone up. Whatever it is to you, do it. Just do it, now. Do not compare your broken vases with anyone else's. In addition, do not break a vase just to outdo someone else. Break a vase for one reason and one reason only, love.

Here is the challenge. Jesus said of the woman that broke the alabaster box that the occasion would be written as a memorial for her. He also said, "She hath done what she could." (Mk. 14:8) Now, you go do likewise. Just do what you can and be quick about it. If you hesitate and try to make reason of it, you will likely not do it. Break a vase for someone today. Make someone say, "I wonder what he is up to." Or, it isn't like her to do such a thing." Make somebody wonder what you are up to and you will have succeeded in breaking a vase.

Beware that as you break a vase, someone in the crowd will be sure to let you know that what you spent or did could have better been done some other way. (Just not by the complainers).

One final thought on this subject. The real vase that needs to be broken is you. We need to give ourselves to one another to help each other through the day. Let us challenge ourselves to make a commitment to be a blessing to each other. Let me illustrate this truth.

In the summer, we often get very thirsty for an ice-cold glass of tea, soda or water. It is common to get the ice cube tray out and fill our glass with ice.

Now, we can be like the ice cube we drop on the floor or like the ice cube in the glass. The difference is the one in the glass is fulfilling the purpose for which it was made. Be like the cube in the glass and allow yourself to "melt" for the betterment of others. You decide to be the one that makes a difference in somebody's life, today. Do it now. Break a vase in your own way.

Break a vase-Write your thoughts

_____

_____

_____

_____

_____

_____

_____

_____

_____

_____

Choices

"The act of choosing; option; a thing or event chosen; to select; to pick or picking; decide or to make a decision; preferences; to choose an option or preference."

We were not able to choose our birth date, nor are we decisive in our death date. However, for most of the days between our birth date and death date, we have the awesome responsibility of making choices. (You could say that the dash on our tombstone represents the choices we made in our life.) Our choices show what we are going after in life. The direction of every human being is determined by what each individual is determined to go after. The choices we make are a reflection of what we go after in life.

We often see or hear such sayings as, "The low price choice", "It's your choice", "The right choice", "The critique's choice", "and the best choice", and so on.

At this time let me mention several rules concerning the making of choices:

A.) Choices have consequences. (Not all consequences are immediate.)

B.) Not choosing is a choice. For instance, not choosing to buy a new pair of shoes is choosing to keep wearing what you have.

C.) In making a choice, you can most often get what you want, but you will also lose what you had. By the way, losing what you had is not always a regretful occasion.

D.) The course of every life is determined by what it goes after. To put it another way, the path we find ourselves on is in direct correlation to our choice.

For instance, Cain made the awful choice to slay his own brother, and in that choice, he lost what he had. Saul made the choice to do away with David, but in making that choice, King Saul lost his peace and later, his throne. Noah made the choice to obey God and build the ark, so Noah and his family did not drown in the worldwide flood.

As creatures with the freedom of choice, we bear a responsibility for our actions. Our actions are in direct relationship to our choices.

This is why we have so many rules and laws. Simply put, we need a reminder when we have made a "bad" choice, such as, going 90 mph in a 70 mph zone. We chose to go beyond the posted speed limit, so we have to bear the consequences of our decision to speed.

However, I must say we should challenge and change some rules that dictate our lives. Case in point, we as Americans should always have the right to bear arms. (I am not talking about the right to wear short sleeve shirts!) Simply put, if we blame the gun for killing, we must also blame the pen for bad checks! We need to make a choice concerning our freedoms as Americans. In addition, we must not allow our freedoms to become an obstacle. This too is a choice.

E.) Not all choices will produce the intended result. If you are a hunter, you may choose to shoot at a rabbit, deer or squirrel with the intended outcome of "bringing it down." Of course, this is not always the case, as you may miss a shot from time to time. It is the same when you swing at a baseball with the intention of hitting it. Or, perhaps you shoot the basketball hoping to score several points. Therefore, in view of the fact that you do not always get the intended results, remember this; you can never hit the ball if you never swing the bat. You can never make a basket you do not shoot. Moreover, you can never bring home the hunted, if you never hunt. You can never win if you do not take the "risk" of losing.

Now the question arises concerning the way we go about making choices in our life. Note the following observations concerning choices.

1) The Path

Choices are often made with the idea of taking or accepting the path of least resistance.

In other words, what is the easiest thing to do? Or, "How can I decide without rocking the boat?" "How can I decide so I will experience the least amount of pain, struggle or conflict?" How can I decide but stay under the radar of resistance?

Or, how can I decide so I will please most of the people affected by my decision? Finally, we often decide in a way that goes along with the crowd, even if it means taking a back seat to what we really believe. "How can I decide and still remain under the radar of criticism?"

2) The Past

Choices are often made according to the results of experience.

For instance, have you chosen to have someone do something for you because he or she did a great job in the past? Or, have you not asked someone to do something for you because the result(s) of the last job was less than satisfactory?

How many times do we make a choice to exclude certain people because of experiences? For instance, how many times have you not asked certain people to help because past experience has taught you that the person or persons has a less than acceptable attitude toward helping or being asked to help. Or, they have a bully sort of know-it-all attitude. They may even scream or holler if they do not get what they want. Or, they may "throw a fit" if they do not hear what they want to hear.

Alternatively, certainly the opposite idea could also exist. You may decide to ask certain people because they are kind and considerate toward you and your needs. They may not always know the answer, but they are always willing to help you find the answer.

We suggested that we often make decisions according to the results of the past. David fought Goliath after he recalled the past and how that God had helped him kill a lion and a bear. Therefore, David concluded in his mind that God would help him fight the giant in the present just as He had helped David fight the lion and the bear in the past. In this case, the past was present in the mind of David but the past cannot be present in reality.

We make decisions according to past success. It may be the way we cook or bake a certain dish. It could be the way certain clothes feel on us, so we make a decision to buy certain brands or styles of clothing. It could be that we have always had good "luck" with certain models of cars or trucks; as a result, we decide to stick with that model or brand.

3) The Promise

Choices are also made according to some sort of Promise that has come your way.

(This is the radio station we all tune to. W I I F M. That is "What's In It For Me?")

For instance, "I promise to pay you such and such amount if you will do a certain job? Therefore, we do the job because we were promised such and such amount. Of course, promises can come in all sorts of forms. "If you will do thus and such, I will promote you to VP of the department." Or, if you take your car this week I will take mine next week." In addition, we could also be making a decision according to the perceived payoff of that decision.

Perhaps the following sort of promise has been used to reward students to study. "Everyone that gets the honor roll this quarter will get a day out of school pass." Therefore, we are taught in early life that <u>if we meet a certain expectation, we will be rewarded</u>. Thus, we learn to make choices according to rewards. However, we may also choose to do something when confronted with a bribe. We have a choice to choose the action connected with the bribe or to reject going along with the bribe.

A reward is given to someone when he or she does something that is good and right in nature. On the other hand, a bribe is given to someone so they will do something wrong or outside of the law or rules set forth.

Surely, it is OK to reward people when they make good choices!

4) The Principle

We also make decisions in accordance to our personal belief system.

In the Bible, the three Hebrew men, Shadrach, Meshach, and Abed-nego decided not to bend nor bow their knee to the Golden image of Nebuchadnezzar the King. The principle is that they would not bow down to, nor worship any graven image. Only the God of heaven is deserving of our worship. (You can read about this in Daniel chapter three of the Holy Bible).

In addition, we were taught certain principles as we grew up. One of the standards or principles we were taught is to make sure we have on clean underwear when we leave the house! Remember those days. We were also taught to treat others, as we would want to be treated. There are standards in your life that may be different from other people of other countries, but we were all taught certain standards of conduct and behavior.

5) The Purse

We make decisions according to the size of our purse. (Financial capabilities)

You surely remember the times when you went to buy something and you had to get a different brand or model because the funds were low! Moreover, perhaps even now you would like to purchase certain items or make certain decisions, but the purse is short a few dollars.

Let me relate a story about this. I recently went to look at a PT Cruiser and ended up taking it for a test drive. Well, as it goes, I drove the Inferno Red, 2002 Limited Edition Cruiser and sort of enjoyed the drive. However, after the salesperson figured out the monthly payment amount, I had to walk off and realize that other things were to take precedence over getting a new PT. I later made a decision to get a Mustang instead.

Far too many people are buying stuff according to the size of someone else's purse. Make sure your decisions fit your purse.

6) The Personality

We make decisions according to our personality or individuality.

For instance, the GT Mustang I bought was red with an automatic transmission. Someone else may prefer to have a silver one with a stick shift. Then again, someone else may want a different type of vehicle altogether, such as a Jaguar. We all have different likes and dislikes. We all have our own individuality. A great part of learning to be you is in making those decisions that fit who you are as an individual and not be concerned in "measuring up" to the standards of someone else. For instance, you have no doubt heard such comments as, "I can't believe you bought that color of car, if it were me, I would not have bought that color." Or, "Are you kidding, did you talk to her at break? I wouldn't talk to her if she was the last person on earth."

Never take a back seat to anybody. You are an individual created by the almighty God. You are not just like anybody else. You are unique. Learn to choose according to your unique likes and dislikes.

And lastly,

7) The Proof

We make decisions or choices according to the "Proof."

What is proof? Proof is evidence, verification, substantiation, a test or experiment that renders a verdict based solely on the facts of the experiment, test or evidence.

At this point, we have to be trained thinkers. If we are to make decisions according to proof, we have to be willing to throw off our own personal ideas, perceptions, prejudices and traditions. This is where we will have to make a conscious effort to look solely at the facts and not allow our feelings or personal preferences to cloud our decisions. We will do ourselves a great deal of good if we learn to ask counsel of other people that have already walked where we are about to go. It is certainly not a disgrace to get good counsel and advice when making some decisions.

Before we bought the house we live in, I had a carpenter look at the house and the structure of it. The carpenter (having had the experience of building houses) advised that it was a good house and in great shape. Buy it. We did.

When buying an appliance, I might do some research or ask other people that already have it, before making the purchase. It is a good idea to research recalls or customer complaints concerning the product you are about to purchase.

The point is, be willing to walk away from a deal if the product or service has been proven to be defective. Do not allow your emotions or feelings to cloud the facts.

In closing, be reminded that we all make choices every day. Some choices are more important that others, but all choices have a certain scope of importance. Whom you marry is a choice that is more important than what you wear to the wedding. How long the wedding ceremony last is not near as important as how long the marriage will last. Where you live is not near as important as how you live. However, where you live could have a bearing on the how.

To choose the cultivating of a good attitude is much more important than aptitude. After all, attitude determines altitude.

We have this marvelous, wonderful, awesome responsibility of choice. Not all of our choices will produce the result we thought. Nor will all of our choices be right. Nevertheless, one thing is certain, in one way or another they are our choices. We have to learn as we go along in life to make better and wiser decisions. Do not get into the paralysis of analysis routine before making a choice. It is certainly admirable to analyze and study before making a choice. However, do not be paralyzed by the fact that it could be a "wrong" choice. Move on if it is a wrong choice and use it as a learning tool in getting on the right path.

Remember, the direction of every life is determined by what it goes after. In addition, keep in mind that we can at any moment chose to go another direction. If you are on the wrong path, decide to get off and start going the right direction.

Go ahead and swing the bat or shoot the ball. Do not keep on waiting for everything to be perfect. Go for it. It is your choice. Now.

Dr. Bob Gerding

Choices-Write your thoughts

_____

_____

_____

_____

_____

_____

_____

_____

_____

_____

_____

_____

_____

_____

_____

_____

Do The Numbers Really Matter?

The first bit of information that we wanted to know about you was in the form of text. "What did you have, a boy or a girl?" The next bit of information was also text related. "What did you name the baby?" After that, it was all numbers.

How much did you weigh? How long was the little one? Five fingers and toes on both hands and feet? What time were you born? On what day was it? From then on, numbers surround you.

The numbers (at least for a big part) have to be watched as you grow. How long did you wait before you took the baby back for a check up? Two weeks, three, or maybe four have passed since birth. Moreover, why would you want to take the little one in for a check up? It was certainly not to make sure the name you have given the child is OK. The reason of course is to check the numbers. How much had the infant grown in the last few weeks. All the vital signs are checked to make sure the numbers are acceptable. Weight and height are checked.

No, you did not wait two or three years before taking the little one back for a check up, but why not? The reason of course is that you wanted to make sure the numbers were all OK. Waiting too long would be taking an unnecessary risk concerning the health of the child. Therefore, you had the numbers checked and continued to do so as the child grew. You do not want to go too long before checking the numbers.

As we move along in life numbers surround us. They are without a doubt a big part of our life. Let me explain what I mean.

From infancy to death, we have a social security number that is part of our identity. Our height, weight, blood pressure, cholesterol levels, heart rate, shoe size, shirt size, pant size, belt size, skirt or bra size are all numbers that tell a story about you. When buying clothes or shoes we want to make certain we select the right number. Not just any number will do! You never just pick one and take it home? No, you look at the numbers. You may even try it on to make sure the number is right for you.

We drive on highways that have number designations. "Yes, we are looking for Route 66." Or, "We have to take I-70 to Interstate 44 and then turn on Highway 98." Moreover, we look at mile markers to make sure we take the right exit.

We buy cars according to the numbers. How many miles is on it, what year of car is it, and how much does it cost? Not to mention, how much will the payment be and for how long? Knowing the numbers will help us make a better decision.

We watch the numbers when we go shopping to buy a ring, a tire, a pair of shoes, a pound of bananas, a big juicy steak, a calling card, diapers, dentures or a double dipped cone. There is no escaping the numbers.

Suppose you were to want to purchase a computer these days. Wow, how many numbers do you need to know to make a smart deal? What is the CPU (Central Processing Unit) speed? How much RAM (random access memory) does it have? What is the speed of the modem? How much memory does the video card have? What is the monitor size and dpi (dots per inch) specification? What is the part number and serial number of the computer? Now, this does not cover all the possible numbers you may want to know before buying a computer but it is a good start. Perhaps the numbers would look like this. The CPU speed is 3.0 gigs. The random access memory is 512 Meg. The modem speed is a 56K modem. The video card memory is 512 Meg. The part number is something like a sixteen digit number. The serial number perhaps is a twelve-digit number. Finally, what version number is some of the software?

Just for fun, jot down some of the numbers in your life and see just how many numbers have been attached to you? Your social security number, house number, telephone number, cell phone number, fax number, time on your watch or clock, age, birth date, shoe size, dress, and skirt or pant size. What about your hat size, belt size, underwear and bra size, shirt size, ring size or waist size? Then we have the numbers that designate the strength of the prescription for your glasses or contacts. What about the number per day and strength of the pills you need to take for an illness. Have we mentioned the number of steps it is up to the front door, to the upstairs bedroom or the steps it will take to go down into the basement? Or perhaps we count the number of windows in your home or car. What about the numbers in your savings or checking account? Not to mention the model or serial numbers of your stove, refrigerator, gun, printer, computer, Pocket PC, Palm, VIN of your car or truck, and the speed limit through your town, down your street or along the express way. Then, you have a license number on your car, your driver's license, a business license number or a membership number. You are in constant touch with your salary amount, number of vacation days, sick days and of course, the number of days before the jerk of the office retires. You are literally surrounded with numbers.

Now, let me explain something else about the numbers in our life. Some of them are changing without your intervention. For example, your age, the numbers of children still at home, (that may take your intervention!), the hairs of your head and your eye prescription.

However, some numbers are changing that we do have some control over, at least, if we take proper steps. How about our weight? Perhaps we can do something to manage and be in control of our weight.

The problem is that we are often so afraid of the numbers we will not get on the scales to find out. We do not want to face it. Now listen, that fear of knowing the number is not keeping you safe. Why do we go through life thinking that a fear can keep us safe? I am not talking about the fear of stepping or running out into traffic. That fear is natural and it does help to keep us safe. I am talking about the fear of keeping up with the numbers in our life. That fear cannot and will not keep you safe. It is so ironic that a boss will keep in touch with the numbers in the office but will not find out his own blood pressure or cholesterol count. You must keep in touch with the numbers in your own personal life. Doing so will show those of your own family that you

31

care about them and that you are willing to take care of the numbers for yourself and for them. It is not enough to know how many hours your crew worked last week or last year. It is not enough to know what time your meetings are. Nor does it matter if you count the hours spent in meetings throughout the year. It is not enough to know the house number or telephone number. You also must take care of your personal numbers such as blood pressure, cholesterol count, weight, HDL, LDL and the other numbers that will help us know our true wellness. This is not something that will accept guesswork. "Oh well, I suppose my weight is just about were it ought to be. I feel fine. In addition, I am relatively sure that my blood pressure and cholesterol count is doing OK. Never mind that it has been several years since I have had them checked." Stop playing with your health. Get the numbers checked. Stop allowing a fear to rule over your health and well-being. That fear will not and cannot keep you safe. Get your numbers checked. Break through that fear and do the right thing for your friend's, family and especially for yourself. Take care of your personal numbers. Knowing your personal numbers will help you live a more satisfying life. Why, because not knowing them will mean that something in your life is incomplete. That incompleteness my friend is a mental weight. Though the weight may be in the recess of your mind, it is still there and you need to deal with it. No matter what we have in our life that is incomplete or unfinished, it is a weight.

Now, here is your prescription. Act upon the truth concerning your numbers. Get them checked. Realize that the fear of knowing the numbers will not keep you safe. This fear of knowing the numbers poses as a friend but is indeed an enemy to your better heath and wealth. Stop fearing the numbers in your own personal life. You be in control of the numbers you can control. Take time today to check your own personal numbers in your life. Get your heath numbers checked. If they are out of bounds, work on getting them where they ought to be for you. This of course may take some time. How about your financial numbers? Come on, get some guts about you and work on those numbers as well.

The numbers in your life do matter. Get them rounded up and all in order. Work on them and do not let them work on you. Who knows, you may save a life, yours. Do your numbers really matter? Of course they do. Get started on them, now.

Do the numbers really matter?-Write your thoughts

_____

_____

_____

_____

_____

_____

_____

_____

_____

_____

_____

_____

_____

_____

_____

_____

Dot To Dot

Remember back in your childhood when you would pick up a book and do the dot-to-dot puzzles. We would trace from one number to the next until we had finished connecting all the numbers. Only after linking all the numbers did we see the finished product. Sometimes it was a cow, horse, bird, house or maybe a flower. Perhaps connecting the dots revealed a picture of a sailboat or fire truck. The point is that as we joined the dots, we did it one number at a time, hopefully in order. Moreover, when we got out of order, we could always stop and get back on track.

Now, allow me to expound upon this simple, yet profound lesson. We would like to take the words "dot to dot" and give them a relevant meaning as to what we are doing in order to finish the picture. <u>D</u>o <u>O</u>ne <u>T</u>hing to <u>D</u>o <u>O</u>ne <u>T</u>hing until you are finished. In other words, connect one dot at a time until the picture is completed. As you connect the dots, connect them in order. However, as the case may have been at times, if you get out of order, stop as soon as you catch it and get back to where you started getting off the path. In addition, no matter if the picture has 23 dots or 104 dots; <u>the only way to completion is to do one thing at a time</u>, connect one dot then the next until completion.

Dr. Bob Gerding

Next time you feel somewhat overwhelmed with too much to do, and your life seems to have too many dots, just remember to take them one at a time.

Stop looking at all the dots and just look and the present one, then the next and the next, until your picture is completed. Do One Thing until the entire project is completed. Stop looking at the forest and see it as one tree. Perhaps it is the springtime chore of cleaning out the garage, or having to get started on a remodeling project, and perhaps, it is nothing more than getting the supper dishes cleaned, do one thing. It may be that you need to balance the checkbook, pay some bills or write a book, it does not matter the object or project, what matters is that we learn to take it one dot and step at a time. Do one thing, that is all. Be in the moment with that one thing.

Have you ever began a project and for some reason or another found yourself beginning to do another? Or, you begin a project and somehow you get off track and begin to do things that will not help you complete the project. For instance, you begin connecting the dots by doing one thing at a time and suddenly you get off track by stopping and getting interested in a show on TV! Now, if it is time for a break and you have connected the amount of dots you set out to connect, then by all means, take a break, just remember where you left off and finish what you set out to do.

Do not be overwhelmed by what is in front of you. Recall that you have finished connecting many dots in the past and that you are well capable to doing it again. Go for it and stay the course. The two most important things about any project are getting started and staying with it until completion. Begin with the first dot until you see the completed picture, by connecting the last dot.

In addition, it may be that you will have the privilege of helping someone else connect the dots as you venture in life, and this is good. Helping others that are overwhelmed is a good reminder for us to see that it is not as bad as it seems, especially, when we help connect one dot at a time. Just remember, that you make it a priority to connect the dots for you and yours. We sometimes use the excuse of helping others so we can get out of making our own picture. Again, we need to help others through life, but we need not use that as an excuse of neglecting our own family and our own self. If you want to see what your picture will look like, you must work on your page.

Remember to do one thing until you see it to completion and once it is finished, you can feel in your heart the satisfaction of another completed project.

Dr. Bob Gerding

Finally, rest a bit and pick up another dot-to-dot puzzle, and imagine what it will turn out to be.

Dot to dot-Write your thoughts

_____

_____

_____

_____

_____

_____

_____

_____

_____

_____

_____

_____

_____

_____

From Now To Was

The only moment any of us will ever have is now. You can never truly be in the past or the future. You can only be in the realm of now. You can only truly be in the present moment. It is true that we can "look into" the past and we can also "look into" the future. Nevertheless, you can never be in the literal past or the literal future. Again, you can only be in the literal now. This literal moment can only be now. So what is was? What does the saying from now to was mean? Now is both constant and fleeting. The passed now is the same as was. Yet, now is present. Because of this, the only way to have a great was is to have a beautiful now. I do not wish to confuse the issue, but be sure that your "was", is not taking precedence over your "now". When you get to was and are "looking" at the past you are at the same time in the realm of now. You have to be in the present to be able to view the past. The truth is that every "now" has a different set of conditions and events, which explains why "was" has a different tune each time we go there to visit. Remember, the only way to have a great "was" is to have a great "now".

From now to was-Write your thoughts

_____

_____

_____

_____

_____

_____

_____

_____

_____

_____

_____

_____

_____

_____

_____

_____

_____

Is There Not A Cause!

The story would not have ended the way it did if he had listened to his elder brother, to King Saul, or allowed the giant to intimidate him.

David would not have defeated Goliath if he had listened to his eldest brother Eliab. The young shepherd boy would not have fought Goliath if he had listened to King Saul's advice. There would be no story of victory for David, if he had followed someone else's "gut".

In I Samuel chapter 17, David's father, Jesse, had given David the task of taking food to his brothers that were in the Army of Israel. As David approached the camp of Israel, he heard Goliath, the great Philistine giant, wagging his tongue and mocking the God of heaven and the Army of Israel. "Come on, let's see if anyone in the camp of Israel can whip me," yelled Goliath as he stood on the other side of the valley. Being six cubits and a span tall (over nine feet tall), we can only imagine that Goliath was a bit intimidating to look at. He did at least intimidate the Army of Israel.

However, David stood without being frightened by the stature or tongue wagging of the giant.

In addition, David was not to be intimidated by the comments of his older brother, Eliab.

"Who have you left those few sheep with" Eliab asked David the shepherd? Eliab continued with his cutting remarks, "I know your pride and the naughtiness of your heart, you have come to the camp of Israel to see the battle." David's reply and recording kept him on track, so he could rise above the "obstacles" of ridicule and fight Goliath the giant.

"Is there not a cause", was the reply of David. His reply came as he looked back into his memory bank and recalled how God had helped him to protect the sheep from a lion and a bear. David replayed the memory tape and encouraged himself in the Lord.

You know the rest of the story. David placed one smooth stone into his slingshot and threw it at the giant. He hit Goliath right in the center of the forehead causing the giant to fall down defeated. David had rocked the giant to sleep. Yet the great question remains for us today as we face our own giants, "Is there not a cause."

What does the phrase "Is there not a cause" really mean?
Is Goliath the giant unconquerable? Is our God unable to oppose him, and subdue him? However, David is not discouraged by the hard, harsh words of Eliab, his brother.
If you are to undertake a service, you must not think it strange, when those from within the camp oppose you. You must respectfully go on with your work, in the face, not only

43

of your enemies' threats, but also of your friend's slights, fears, ridicule and censorship.

Has there been a time in your life, when you set out to do something and there was someone willing to let you know that it was a crazy idea, and that you had better not take any chances. No matter what you do in life there will always be "Negavites" to let you know it cannot be done.

Look back and see the great accomplishments of the past. See how many people overcame adversity, ridicule, and being made a spectacle in their day. For example, the steamboat, airplane, light bulb, automobile, and telephone were all born in travail. Nothing is ever accomplished as long as we listen to those that are not willing to do it themselves.

Noah built the ark as he was commanded of God. I really believe that the people in his day thought Noah was some sort of a nut. However, Noah and his family kept on building and preparing for what would eventually happen. A worldwide flood such as we have never seen since the days of Noah had come upon the people in that day.

Also, know that whatever your mission, you are responsible to see it to completion. It may not be a multi-million dollar project, but that is not the point. The point is that you are responsible for your mission.

For instance, suppose your mission at this point of your life is to see that your brothers and sisters get back together and become the family you once were. However, that may never happen if you keep making excuses and let fear of failure keep you down. Get up and just do it. The greatest deterrent in getting involved in helping others is fear. We are afraid we will make things worse. Or, we will not succeed in our endeavor to help.

It may be, that something at the work place needs to be changed, but you are afraid that "they" will say, "That's how we have always done it, if it isn't broke don't fix it!" Are you afraid of the rejection? Do not be. Just do something to get the ball rolling and stay at it. Is there not a cause to make a difference in the work place, home place, church place and earth place? Dare to do something beneficial today. Now. Is there not a cause?

Go ahead, dare to stand up and be counted as being different. Dare to be like the leader of a great orchestra and turn your back to the crowd. Go ahead and direct that great piece of work in your life. When the audience applauds, be sure to stand aside and show off the orchestra that helped to bring a beautiful work together.

Your piece of work may be a building program. Whether a doghouse or church house, it does not matter. What matters is that you get a vision for what you can do, ask God for guidance, pray, and get to work. It is time to have a passion and a cause in your life.

Is there not a cause for what you have on your heart at this very moment! Great things are not accomplished by wishing, hoping or by constantly doing nothing but analyzing. You must see that you have a cause and be willing to stick with the stuff until completion. Be willing to make a difference.

Perhaps, your mission is to see that a relationship has recaptured harmony and peace. Your mission may be to see that a family in need receives the aid that will help them along the way. It may be, someone within your reach is down and out and that person has a need for a friend to help him (or her) along life's journey. It may be that you feel an issue at church, work or home needs to be discussed and worked out, go for it. It may be an issue in your community, city, county, state or country. You be that person. Make a difference. Dare to be different. Is there not a cause?

The giants of life are there to be conquered. Remember, you and God are a majority. David went to meet the giant head on. He did not go in fear, but in a passion to slay the giant and rock him to sleep.

What are the giants in your life? Is it mending a relationship? Perhaps a building program is your giant. Speaking up in the work place, home place, or church place to make a difference may be a hurdle you find hard to jump. We all have giants to defeat in our lives. Some of the giants we face are the physical giants in our life such as illness and pain. It may be a financial giant. Perhaps a social giant keeps you locked up. There is a way out. If you do not believe there is a way out, then, there is a way through. As David faced the giant, face yours. If you read the story, you will find that David ran toward the giant. He went forward to defeat the giant. Go forward sir. Go forward madam. Go forward young child, teacher, preacher, parent, worker and all. As you go forward, remember those words of David the mighty shepherd,

<u>Is there not a cause?</u>

Is there not a cause!-Write your thoughts

_____

_____

_____

_____

_____

_____

_____

_____

_____

_____

_____

She Hath Done What She Could

In breaking a vase, we read that the woman had done what she could. We see in Mark chapter fourteen and verse nine (Mk.14:9) that the occasion is marked as a memorial of the woman.

Let us look at the philosophy drawn from the statement, "she hath done what she could".

Why would the Lord render this occasion as a memorial? Why make a big deal over this woman doing what she could do? People always expect us to do what we can.

We know this occasion to be the Anointing at Bethany. The fact that Jesus was anointed makes this occasion special and worthy of our consideration.

So often, we do not think it necessary to praise and encourage someone for doing what they can. So why should we even consider it? We will look at five different reasons that we need to be a good finder, even in the "little things" as we do what we can.

(1) First of all, doing what you can is often dull or dreary. There are no banners flying in the sky overhead. No parade with a drummer playing our favorite tune as a marching

band goes down the street. When we do what we can, in taking out the trash, for example, there will likely not even be any consideration to think the act to be praise worthy. On the other hand, if hubby forgets to take out the trash, he is in deep trouble for his error. Doing what we can is often unexciting.

(2) Secondly, doing what you can often goes unnoticed. This is because doing what you can must be your responsibility and duty. In addition, doing what you can should be understood as being a small piece of the whole puzzle.

We all know that the work place which hands out praise for doing what we should is rare to find. Yet, if a small thing goes wrong, you are most assured that you would hear about it and perhaps be penalized, disciplined, or warned.

If you happen to be in management, read the next few sentences carefully. One of the five basic needs of human kind is appreciation. From an economic point of view, showing appreciation will earn you more money than if you do not practice appreciation. It is time to become more aware of those people that are faithful in doing what they can and letting people know that you caught them being faithful.

Let me give an example. Suppose you are a manager and that, you require a weekly report. It would make more sense to encourage people as they faithfully hand in their reports. If that is the case and it makes sense, why do those in charge try to motivate by using a negative reprimand? "If you don't hand in a report next week, you are going to be written up." It may even be advisable to find out why the report remains an unfinished task...

So far, we see that doing what we can is unexciting and unnoticed.

(3) Now, we will see that doing what we can is normally unspectacular.

There are no fireworks to light the night sky because you took out the trash or because the child made her bed and cleaned her room. There will not be a crowd to gather because you did a good job in the office or assembly line.

Why do I even give this article consideration? Simply and honestly put, I am trying to inspire you to become abnormal. Dare to be different, much different from the normal. In my own experience as a Quality Control Inspector (several moons ago), it was normal for me to speak well of line workers when "I caught them" doing a good job. This was done on an individual basis as well as when people worked together as a team. It was common for me to hear such comments as, "I'm glad somebody notices that I am doing what I can, the boss sure doesn't seem to notice. That is, until somebody on the production line "drops the ball".

By the way, when you are in the habit of being a good finder, it is easier for people to accept it when you have to tell them if they need to do a better job.

(4) In addition, doing what we can is often unappreciated and (5) unacknowledged by anyone.

By the way, if everything you do is unexciting, unnoticed, unspectacular, unappreciated and unacknowledged, you still need to learn from the experience and make sure that you give to others that which you would like to receive. Just do what you can, where you can, and when you can.

Too often, we want to give the $50,000.00 we do not have instead of giving the $5.00 or $50.00 that we do have. Just do what you can, where you can, when you can. My grandmother Jones told me years ago, "Every feller knows his own business best". That is, you are the one that will know if you can give the $5 or the $50 or perhaps, even the $50,000.00. Many would like to write the next best novel or article in the paper, but will only wish about it. You can however, without a doubt, write a beautiful note of encouragement or send a brief note of appreciation to someone.

Let me pass on an idea. You be a leader in noticing what others do as they do what they can. Catch someone doing something right and let them know it. You might even want to do something unusual for them. As my children were growing up, I occasionally would get them out of bed and surprise them by taking them out to get an ice cream cone. Do something different.

I am not saying that you need to "gush" all over people. Yet, we need to do what we can and encourage people to do what they can. "Do unto others as you would have them do unto you"., and try to be first.

Go ahead, be the first in the work place, church or home to make a difference, as you are a good finder.

She has done want she could in that she broke a vase.

The lad gave his lunch of five loaves and two small fishes. The widow gave her mite. And you, you will give? What? Dare to be different. Now.

She hath done what she could-Write your thoughts

_____

_____

_____

_____

_____

_____

_____

_____

_____

_____

_____

_____

_____

_____

_____

_____

The Dash

You have seen it many times in many different formats. Some times the dash (-) is used in dates such as 1-27-1903. At other times, you may use the dash as a means to give a computer file a name such as "My-Files". Perhaps the dash helps to write up a part number, 105-27-195. We know that most telephone books will use a dash to separate the number sequence such as 111-222-3456

In this chapter, I would like to take a moment to explain that we often overlook the dash. We also forget what it stands for.

If you were to walk through any cemetery, you would see the dash I am talking about on just above every stone. For instance, most every tombstone is marked with a date of birth and date of death. In between most birth and death dates, there is a separator, the dash.

Now think about the dash and the meaning of it. What is the focus of the dash? It seems to me that the dash represents the life of the individual from birth to death.

Now, let us get it down to detail. It is not just life as an accumulation of years but also a life as an accumulation of events within those years. It represents all the memories we may have of someone. It is the life story of every human being. It is the now when the now was then. Remember that a great now will result in a great was.

My advice to you is to learn to build a great now. Keep building and experiencing the now in the best way possible and you will be able to leave a life with a great was. However, a great was will be accomplished with knowing how to live now, in the present. We must be learning to make the most of every situation. Learn to be in the now.

Believe me, some day my dash will come. Some day your dash will come. What will that dash represent to those left behind? Your dash will be the story you left with your actions, words, writings, habits, and just being you.

I often go to the cemetery and visit my relative's graves. As I look at the stone and see the dash between the dates, I think about the time the dash represents.

With grandpa, I think about the times I mowed his lawn as he sat on the porch and watched. I also think about how he would buy, sell and trade with other people in order to make a buck or two. With grandma, I think about the great meals she prepared and all that she did for me. With my dad, I think about all his hard work and the times he took us to church. Of course, there are friends as well as relatives that we think about as well. I think about a man that I use to work with in the factory. When I see his dash, I think of all the times we talked together in the work place.

You see, your dash will tell some sort of story to somebody. Your story reveals your choices. How will others read your dash? How will my children and relatives read my dash? Does it matter? Well ask yourself this question if you wonder that. "What do you wish you could have said about someone else's dash?" Do you think someone may someday say that about your dash? Then yes, it does matter.

It is not a matter of perfection in life. It is just a matter of life. Listen, most of us need more life in our living. Make your dash tell a story that others can laugh about, cry about and be thankful about. Make your dash a story that will proudly be told to others as they grow up and look over your pictures. Pictures are a good way of explaining the dash. Take plenty of them.

Now let me say this before leaving this chapter. It may be that as you look at the dash of a friend or relative that you have a taste of disgust or regret. If so, learn from that but do not let it dominate your life. The dash on the tombstone may scream abuse at you. It may tell a story of neglect and pain. Learn from it. Do not see it as permanent. Go beyond that and grab a hold of its lesson. Use it to make your dash better.

Dr. Bob Gerding

Remember, we are all going to bear a dash on our own stone. What will your dash mean to those you leave behind? Make now to be a great was. Now.

The dash-Write your thoughts

The World's Oldest Game
(That is not really a game)

If you were to do some research on what the world's oldest game is you would no doubt agree with my suggestion? Let us look at a scenario into what we known as the oldest game in the world, which is not really a game at all. Read on and learn as you go.

The sternness of his face was an indication that he was speaking his mind with passion and urgency. "No, it's not my fault, so don't blame me for what she did. She was the one that caused the whole thing".

Here we see the beginning of what has been termed as the "blame game" among us earthlings. Adam was the first to use the famous saying. He blamed the woman. "It's not my fault God; it's that woman you gave me. She is the one that plucked the fruit off of the tree, took a big juicy bite and then stuck it in my mouth".

It is a blame game that is not really a game at all. Adam was serious. He felt it was only reasonable to want to protect himself against such serious charges. "Who did this", was the question God asked of Adam? The answer then is the same as it is now, "Don't blame me; it was you know who that did it". Adam is now speaking from the voice of fear and protection. Now, let us look at the operation and features of blame.

First, we must answer the question, "what is blame"? In addition, how did blame get its first breath of life?

According to the dictionary, blame is the act of finding fault. It is the act of accusing someone to be guilty. It could be that we would take the blame in order to protect someone else. On the other hand, we may blame someone else in order to protect ourselves. Either way, blame has a thick layer of protective coating all over it. Blame is the armored car that protects its contents.

We all have resorted to blame at one time or another. Remember those words as a youth, "It wasn't my fault, he made me get into the cookie jar. He made me take the lid off, stick my hand in there, and get a cookie. He forced my mouth open and caused me to eat the chocolate chips. While I chewed the cookie, he looked at me and it caused me to swallow. It is not my fault the cookie has found a resting place in my stomach! He made me do it." Blame him.

As I work in the corporate world, I sometimes wonder if blaming and accusing are worse among "adults" than it is with children! We expect children to resort to blame because they are immature. They feel the need to protect themselves. Yet, so many adults feel it is easier to use blame and accusations rather than accept personal responsibility. After all, adults have an image to keep intact! Adults will often do whatever it takes to protect their image. I feel that the basic reason we use blame is to protect ourselves, or in some cases, we may desire to protect someone else so we accept the blame.

It is so immature for a boss (or person of authority) to use the instrument of blame in order to justify the situation as they see it. Let me give you an example.

Suppose I have a boss and his name is Timmy. Timmy has a boss and his name is Dave. Of course, Dave has a boss, and his name is Leon. Leon discovers a problem within the company and gets very upset. Leon in turn goes to Dave about the problem. Of course, Dave is not going to take the blame or the heat so he goes to Timmy and hands him the hot potato of retribution and blame. In turn, Timmy gets angry and begins to yell and scream (this helps him get his point across in a mature way!) and lets me know that I am to blame for this whole mess and that I had better get it straightened out in short order, or else! In order to release my anger for unjust blame, I go home and kick my cat out of the house. It would have been easier if Leon had come to my house and kicked the cat instead.

Do you see what is happening here? The main concern at this point is to blame someone else so we can protect the image we have of our position and ourselves. In this scenario, it looks as if the main goal is to protect ourselves first and solve the problem second. It is as if someone has to bear the blame before we can solve the problem. For some reason we believe that, we have to prove that we are right and someone else screwed up.

Listen, it is time that some adults grow up and stop hiding behind their positions, possessions and power. What a pitiful bunch of human beings we have become. We have not yet learned that blaming is part of a child's world. It is so ironic that we can see through children when they resort to blaming others. Yet, we as adults do not face ourselves. Hypocrite, you have deceived yourself. You prove that you wish to live the lie of a child. You wish to live in the child's world of immaturity.

What would be the responsible thing to do with blame? Let us use the scenario of Leon, Dave, Tim and myself that we used earlier. Because we are all a part of the same company, would it not make logical and common sense to want to help each other on the team rather than tear one another down? It would be better to attack the situation and problem than to attack each other. Why not simply get together (as adults) and work things out. Forget about protecting yourself and learn to do what is best to protect the team and your company from the competition, (the other companies that wish to sink your business). Learn to get off the playground of your feelings, possessions and position and work together to build a great team. I think we forget that we are on the same team! Let us accept our part of responsibility. Let us realize that it is not required that we find someone to blame for the way things are. I do declare that some people act as if it is their full time job to locate someone to blame. They will spend more time searching for someone to blame than they will in finding a solution to the problem. In fact, if they can blame someone, they feel as if they have found a solution. Hey, grow up.

Next, we will understand that blaming carries with it the following ten observations.

1) Blame seeks company. The immature person that receives blame must find someone else to blame as well. The domino effect goes from the top down. It can and often goes in a horizontal manner from one coworker towards another, such as "I would be able to get my work done, but my coworker just won't help me." It may be that you just need to show up for work instead of trying to blame someone else for not getting your work done. Stop hiding behind blame.

2) Blame seeks to blame and then leaves the scene to watch what happens next. It wishes to cover its tracks as if it were never around. (Then blame hides to watch.)

3) Blame seeks to clear its name before you discover the truth.

4) Blame seeks to protect itself while exposing someone else.

5) Blame seeks to strangle the life out of responsibility and send it away gasping for breath.

6) Blame seeks to be number one on our top ten lists of solutions.

7) Blame seeks to be the Sheriff, Judge, Jury, Defense attorney, and Prosecutor. In addition, blame walks around as if to be the "Good Guy".

8) Blame dresses in a finely pressed dress suit so the mud it slings will appear clean.

9) Blame seeks to appear strong because it is weak.

10) Blame seeks to take you on a path contrary to responsibility and truth.

The real question remains, what will you do with blame. Do not allow yourself to take the road that Adam took. Step back, look at the situation, and get to work on a solution. Let us learn to work as a team. Now.

The World's Oldest Game-Write your thoughts

_____

_____

_____

_____

_____

_____

_____

_____

_____

_____

_____

_____

_____

_____

_____

_____

_____

Under Siege

The morning is calm as the sun begins to peek over the horizon. There is a light breeze in the air as the bushes sway from side to side, gently and joyfully. The tranquil wind is playing with the bushes in the quiet calm of the morning. The birds sing their usual song of gratefulness and joy. "It's another day of life, and we're glad to be a part of it." The morning is so quiet that the bright sunrays give off a silent sound of laughter. Sunbeams dance across the morning sky skipping towards the boundaries of the earth and finally crawl through the curtains to reach the corner of your eyes. Even though there is tranquility and serenity on the outside, inside is a completely different story.

It starts very early in the morning while you are still lying in bed and begins suddenly, without warning. You are under siege before you can even blink an eye. As that first sunbeam crawls upon your bed, darkness begins to dominate in your mind.

As soon as you awake, there is a war going on inside your head. There are at least fifty or more thoughts shooting about inside your mind wounding you before you even have a chance to take cover, even though you are under the covers.

There they are, just as they have been for the last few years of your life. There is this battle in your mind as you awake to another day.

One thought after another rages trying to make sure that you are defeated and wounded in the day before giving you a chance to start the day. Feelings and thoughts are attacking you vigorously. You do your best to shake it. The more you argue with your thoughts, the worse the battle becomes.

Then, you bravely plant your feet firmly on the floor and walk into the kitchen to get the usual morning coffee. Nevertheless, before you know it, you are under attack again. They are all over you; those self-defeating thoughts are back again. (Did they ever leave)?

The thoughts you are having are telling you that you will never make it today. That the meeting you planned will go wrong; that the traffic will be so bad you will probably be late for work. Thoughts keep coming as if to be trying to get you down before you have a chance to get up. Thoughts and feelings about your appearance and intelligence flood over you trying to drown your being and suffocate the life and zeal from you. Then, thoughts about the boss haunt you. The reports that are due, the unpaid bills, the upcoming appointments, the present, the future and yes, even the past. Oh, do not forget about the "What If" monster that follows your shadow. You think of the children at college, about a jerk of a co-worker, a planned meeting for today, scheduling conflicts over the holidays two months from now, and finally yet importantly, thoughts about what everybody else must be thinking about you? You may also struggle about your weight or the clothes that you wear. "Will I be able to please everybody today", you ask yourself. "What will people think of me, my car, my house, my report, my sermon, my lesson or my suggestions at the meeting"? "Am I up with the rest of the pack"? This is exhausting. I am exhausted before I even get to work!

Help, I am under siege by my own thoughts and feelings. They have me held captive and I am nearly ready to surrender as an unworthy hostage.

It is as if I have become a servant to my thoughts and feelings instead of my thoughts and feelings serving me. Are my thoughts and feelings really supposed to be the master of my life? On the other hand, am I supposed to be the master of my thoughts and feelings? Am I really supposed to continue on this course of life with all these self defeating thoughts and feelings"? Are my thoughts and feelings supposed to be working for me and not against me? Perhaps it would be better if I just stayed in bed a little bit or maybe even a lot longer. Maybe the thoughts would retreat, at least for a little while. If I sleep more, perhaps I will have the thoughts less. So it seems. Is this why we want to run to sleep sometime? Who is responsible for giving me the capability and capacity to have thoughts and feelings? Is this the doing of man, or is this the divine plan of a higher being, a higher power, God? Yes of course, God gave me this wonderful gift of thought and feelings. He did not give them to me so they could stomp on me every morning, noon and night, and throughout the day. He gave me the capacity to think and feel in order that thought and feeling might be a servant and not a master. In order that thought and feeling might serve.

I recall times that I have used thought to make a decision that I truly believed was right and proper. Yet, after making the decision, Dr. Thought and Professor Feeling presented themselves to me and mocked the decision that I had made earlier. My thoughts have turned against the decision they had helped me make. What is up with this? This is not the first time this has happened. My own thoughts and feelings are against me! No matter what I decide and no matter how long it takes me to make the decision, once I have decided, my thoughts present themselves to me and begin the grueling interrogation. My thoughts then scream at me, "Are you sure"? "Why did you make that decision and not take the other option"? "Are you kidding, only a loser would have decided the way you did"? "Just what do you think the others will say about your decision"? The thoughts relentlessly attack me. I then ask myself, "Is this the same mind that helped me to make the initial decision"? I now realize that I am under siege and have barely begun a new day. I have not even had a chance to get the bacon and eggs on to fry.

If I could only discover the truth and rid myself of these self-defeating thoughts and feelings I would be so grateful. Why do my own thoughts turn against me? Why do my thoughts and feelings help me make a decision and then do an about face and tromp on me for making the decision?

Let me illustrate this scenario. You are getting ready to retire for the evening and you get a phone call from someone asking you for a favor. As a good friend, you agree to help because you think it is the right thing to do. You then decide to go on to bed. As soon as you wake up, your thoughts are pouncing on you for making the decision the night before. You have about twenty or so thoughts that are telling you what a nut you are for agreeing to do what you said you would do. It seems to be one inner battle after another. What is happening here?

It is the committee. The ever-elusive self-appointed committee has come back to wreck and haunt you. Be aware that the "committee" is that part of you that is ever seeking for the approval of your decisions and actions from someone else. It is seeking approval from outside of you. You know this is true when you begin asking yourself some questions. Such as, "What will dad or mom think about this?" "Will my co-workers still be my friends if I go on a 3 or 4 day vacation"? "What will the people at church say about me"? You see, you do not know it, but you are constantly seeking for approval outside of yourself. It is in some way something we do to protect our image as we imagine it to be in the eyes of others. "I must always be pleasing and approved by others" is our secret thought. "Everybody at church or work must always approve of me" is our thought. We are afraid. Afraid that we will not project an image that we feel others expect of us. It is at this point that we are seeking for that crumb of approval from outside of ourselves. We strive to rid ourselves of rejection. Our constant goal is to make it through another day without being criticized by our peers. We fervently seek to be acceptable and praised by our peers. We go to great lengths to make sure we are right. You must learn when to dismiss the committee and pay no attention to it and when to obey the committee and do its bidding. What is the difference and how do you decide which committee to listen to and which one to dismiss? Very simply, do what is true. We are constantly looking outside of ourselves for approval. We seek to protect the image we wish to project.

We know what to say to certain people to make sure they approve of us? It is also true, that this is exactly what we do whether or not we really believe what we are saying. Too many people have become "justified" professional liars. We strive to make sure that others approve and accept us. At the same time, we compromise what we really believe. The truth is, you are grasping onto and clinging to someone else's truth. You are living a lie life so you can "fit in" and receive your crumbs.

You know those people in your life that vacillate from one opinion to another! Sure, you think that the color green is awful until your new boss loves it. Then, when you get a different boss (or other significant being) in your life, you seem to figure out that what you really hated was a different color altogether. You adjust in every way needed to make sure you are on the "winning" side. What you do not realize is that this in itself makes you a loser. Stop being a waffler and a flip-flop. Start to baffle people by being yourself. If you dislike the color green, then dislike it. Do not be sensitive as to whether someone else may think you odd for not liking the color green. It is just a color. Move beyond this.

Get off the board of this committee. Dismiss yourself from it. It is time you were OK with you and your preferences so long as your preferences do not violate the laws of nature and God.

Allow me to illustrate further. You may not like Mustangs. That is OK. I do. That is OK. It is only a car. I will not allow you to take this away from me. Neither should you allow me to take away from you the car or vehicle of your choice. It should not bother you that I really do not care for some other vehicles. I will not wake up tomorrow morning wondering why you do not like Mustangs, at least not to the point that it causes me to wage a battle in my own mind about it. I do not base my likes and dislikes of vehicles (or anything else) based on your criteria. If I had my way about it (and I could afford it), I would have a brand new bright red Cobra Mustang with automatic transmission and premium sound system with low profile tires and tinted glass. Should I put my mind on the hat rack along with my hat and use your mind for my life? My Mom use to say, "God gave you a head to be used for more than a hat rack."

The question remains, how do I stop the committee? How do I wake up in a different manner? What is the prescription to wake up ready for another day of challenges with confidence and vitality? How do I take back my mind from the committee? How do I wake up ready for the challenge of another day instead of the dread?

1. Replace the committee.

2. You hire a different committee and name it Truth.

3. Stop the old committee tapes from replaying and start playing a different tape. Your tape. Baby steps will do. Just get going in the right direction.

4. Don't Quit.

5. Seek what is true. Seek to live now.

6. Stop allowing your mind to be central to its own self. You be in charge of your mind and not your mind in charge of you. Smile at your mind from time to time.

7. Seek to put in your mind those things that will make it healthy. Stop the garbage dump thinking. This could include jealousy, bitterness, and other such thoughts. If you had a million dollar horse, would you feed it just anything? You are certainly worth more than a million dollar horse.

8. Realize that most of the time we are on the defensive. We work overtime at protecting ourselves from the questionable or disapproving opinions of others. We seem to deny ourselves the right to be ourselves. We work at "fitting in" so we can get the approval we strive to receive. God's approval will do.

Come awake to the truth. Forget about tradition and the norm. What is the truth? The truth shall make you free.

9. Every morning as you awake, imagine that you are attending a ribbon cutting ceremony. It is the beginning of a new day and you get to cut the ribbon. Enjoy the new day that the ribbon cutting introduces. Once the ribbon cutting ceremony is complete, go ahead, step out, and believe. No matter what day of the week it may be, neither you nor I have been here before nor shall we ever be here again. Understand that each new day is another Grand Opening to experience life. Also, remember that today is not a practice session. This is it.

10. Prepare for another ribbon cutting ceremony the night before it is to happen. Remember, you are a winner and you will mount up as wings of eagles. Go ahead and soar above the crowd. Now.

Under Siege-Write your thoughts

_____

_____

_____

_____

_____

_____

_____

_____

_____

_____

_____

_____

_____

_____

_____

Watch What You Say When You Talk To Yourself!

Have you ever been overheard talking to yourself, and be asked who you were talking to? Then, the reply we hear next is that it is all right to talk to yourself as long as you do not answer yourself back.

The estimation is that we have 45 to 55 thousand thought sessions of talking to ourselves per day. If that were the case, this would amount to 2200 sessions an hour, or 36 per minute. It has been estimated that about 80% to 90% of our self-talk is done as a picture thought (visual) and not words. Of this, some 75% of our picture thoughts are negative.

For instance, have you ever had someone tell you that, "so and so" said you were a stupid idiot, ugly, crazy, or some other cutting remark? Alternatively, it  may be that you have told yourself such things. As soon as you hear the statement, most of us get a picture in our minds of the announcement. The next time we encounter the person, we tell ourselves (in pictures) that ole "so and so" thinks I am an idiot. Hence, we begin seeing ourselves as idiots, or whatever the suggestion was that came bursting into our thoughts. The danger lies in the fact that we so often replay the tape repeatedly in our minds until it seems almost impossible to erase. As we see it in our mind, it is not in alphabet or sentence form, but rather in the form of a picture of how we must appear while acting, looking or being stupid, according to ole "so and so."

The fallacy of all this is that none of this has a bases of fact or truth. You are not an idiot, stupid, or ugly. You are a unique individual. There is not another  one like you on the face of the earth, anywhere. If "so and so" wants to think that way, fine, let him, go ahead and live a miserable life, but do not allow him to drag you down to his level. Erase the tape immediately. It is a problem for "so and so" to deal with, not you. Do not replay those words in your head again. Cast them off and replace them with truth. You are a unique individual, not made according to the will of man, but rather according to the will of God. Sure, you may not know it all, but who does? You may not be able to do everything, but you can do something. You will get it wrong occasionally, but join the club, because we all get it wrong sometime. You may not always shine forth as the sun at midday, so what. What is so wrong with being a star that shines through the darkness at night? Is that not a beautiful site?

Let me now relay to you a true story about a man that let his mind pictures destroy his life. It is a story that the scriptures tell about a man named Saul. This happens to be one of the saddest stories in scripture. It depicts the truth of how, if we are not careful, we can begin to allow our thought(s) to control us, rather than work at getting an understanding of the truth and learning to control our thoughts. The story is in First Samuel chapter seventeen. (I Sam.17)

A young shepherd boy named David obeyed his father and went to the battlefield in the valley to take food to his older brothers. While in the camp, David heard Goliath the giant yelling out threats and mocking the God of heaven. The threats of Goliath were like chains of bondage to the army of Israel. No one in the camp, except for a shepherd boy named David was willing to go and fight the giant.

The young shepherd began to replay a story about how in the past, he had killed a bear and a lion as they tried to make a meal of some of the sheep he was watching over. He (David) was recalling how God had been there to help him in the past. David was telling a true story by using word pictures to convey what had happened. He was not living the past, but rather recalling it in his mind. He was using the experience to help him now.

At this point of the story, King Saul put his own armor on David and instructed him to go and fight the giant. David had not needed this armor to fight the bear or the lion, so he took it off and laid it aside. It just did not fit. David then reached for his slingshot, picked up five smooth stones from the cool brook and placed them in his leather pouch. Now, to make a short story long, we know that David placed one smooth stone into his sling shot, wound up for the throw, and hit Goliath right smack dab in the center of the forehead. This one stone rocked the giant to sleep, dead asleep. David had won the battle and the armies of Israel chased down the Philistines.

It was then that King Saul learned more about David and put him in charge of the armies of Israel.

So far, the story has revealed to us a sweet victory over the enemy of Israel  and the beginning of a great relationship

between David and King Saul. Yet, as we will see, Goliath was a smaller enemy of David.

As King Saul and the men of war marched into the homeland, the women were in the streets singing a victory song. The song had a part in it that said, "Saul has slain his thousands, but David has slain his ten thousands." Upon hearing this, King Saul was bothered very badly with pictures in his mind as he said to himself, "What can he (David) have more but the Kingdom." In other words, King Saul got a picture in his mind of David stepping up to the throne as King. From that day forward, King Saul sought to kill David.

It was not the words the women sang that caused King Saul to become jealous of David. Rather, it is Saul's perception of the words and the picture he gave to the words. Saul is responsible concerning his reaction to what he heard. Day after day, Saul replayed the tape of the victory song in his head. He saw David as a foe rather than as a friend. He saw David as King rather than a conqueror.

Watch what you say when you talk to yourself. Put a harness on your imagination and control it rather than allowing your imagination to put a harness on you. The imagination is to be a servant and not the master.

How many of us have said something like "I know I am going to get sick again this November. I seem to always get a bad cold right after Thanksgiving." Guess what, the mind of man wants to be right and we often do what we have to in order to prove that we are right. "See, I told you I would be sick after thanksgiving, it happens every year." We see ourselves being sick. We use pictures when we say,

"I remember last year when I got sick about this time and here I am again, sick, just like last year."

What about the statement we make after the interview. "I knew the interview would go bad, they always do." I remember my last interview was not too good either." Even in sports, we talk to ourselves, "See, I told you I was going to strike out again. I just cannot hit the ball in a real game. I seem to do really good in practice, but when it comes to the real game, I always strike out."

Listen, why not look at the real game as another practice session and go ahead and hit the ball. Stop telling yourself what you do not want to do and get a picture of what you need to do and can do.

How about the unwise coach that chews out the team by telling them they are always missing free throws, which have caused the team to lose. Then he so "wisely", proceeds to make them run laps as a way of punishment. Will running really make you a better free throw shooter? It seems to me that it will make you a better runner! Practicing free throws I think would help more.

Why not say to the team "free throws are often the difference between winning and losing a game. Now, let us get some practice in at the free throw line. You hit 63% last game but I think you can get at least 75% or better at our next game"

Encourage by letting them know what you want them to do, not by what you don't want them to do. Give them a picture that encourages them to excel. Give them a goal to shoot for within the game, a higher percentage of shots made from the free throw line.

Here is another way to say it. "The direction of every life is determined by what it goes after." "We are guided by and go towards our most current dominant thoughts." Therefore, the fact of the matter is that we often get sick not because of what we have eaten, but rather because of what is eating us. You have to ask, "what we are feeding our minds."

Now, before I finish this chapter, I must ask you a question. What is it that you have been telling yourself? What lies are you repeatedly going over? Could it be that you have been telling yourself some of the following lies?

I must be perfect in order to be accepted! That is a lie.

Everyone must like me! That is a lie. I must seek the approval of everyone! That is a lie. If I make a mistake, it is because I am worthless! That is a lie. I must be very capable in every situation! That is a lie. These are all lies.

Watch what you say when you talk to yourself. Learn not to jump to conclusions, but rather be learning to jump to solutions. Remember that you are a unique individual placed upon this earth by the wisdom and plan of God. You are not a mistake. You are a precious soul and being.

Watch what you say when you talk to yourself. Stop living a lie. Stop being your own doormat. Be careful of the mental pictures you paint for yourself and others. Paint with true color on a white canvas.

Begin again. Now.

Dr. Bob Gerding

Watch what you say when you talk to yourself!
Write your thoughts

_____

_____

_____

_____

_____

_____

_____

_____

_____

_____

_____

_____

_____

When Silence Screamed
(And no one listened)

It was a day that started out full of beauty and tranquility. The birds whistled songs of peace and joy as they frolicked from tree to tree and bush to bush. The wind blew gently against the lion's mane as she played with a baby cub on the green plush carpet of earth. The fruit trees smiled as they turned their face to the sun and made a "thumbs up" sign towards heaven. Great and small fish of the sea made a giant circle eight while making sure not to crash into one another at the intersection of the circle eight. It was a picture perfect day in paradise for the one man and one woman that inhabited the earth, Adam and Eve.

It was on this peaceful day that silence first screamed but no one heard its voice. Let us see what happened that day in the garden, and as we do, understand that this phenomenon is still happening today. Listen to the story we have titled, "When Silence Screamed".

There they were, together in the most beautiful place on earth, the Garden of Eden. It was a place of absolute bliss and peace. A place of Perfection, without flaw, confusion, or instant anything. Adam and Eve lived in such a flawless time that even their nakedness enhanced the setting. Yet, that was all about to change.

Of all the trees in the garden, they had no boundaries except for one. That one tree was not to have the fruit of it eaten. All the other trees in the garden were perfect in their produce and taste. Yet, this one tree was the place of temptation. It is like having a sign on a park bench that says "Wet Paint-Do Not touch". We want to test the boundaries in our lives. Therefore, we look around to see if anyone sees us. We lean over and barely touch the painted surface. In touching it, we discover that we had crossed the boundaries and had in the process, gotten our finger wet with fresh paint. We also leave our fingerprint in the paint. We leave a mark of crossing over the boundary.

In the Garden of Eden, we see the dramatic outcome of crossed over boundaries and the result of silence.

The devil had come to the Garden that day to tempt Eve and get her to partake of the fruit from the forbidden tree. "Just touch it, he remarked, "smell it, feel it, taste it, and you will see that it will be good for you."

All the while, we hear the blood-curdling scream of silence trying to get the attention of the man, Adam. Standing there by Eve, Adam managed to keep total silence, while Eve did the talking and dealing with the serpent. Silence was screaming and trying to get Adam to speak up. "Speak up Adam," said silence as it pressed against his conscience. "Speak up Adam", before the serpent causes Eve to go over the edge and violate God's clear command, "Do not partake of the fruit of the forbidden tree". "Adam, this is a time that I am not golden" said Silence with urgency. "Speak man; do not allow this to go on without speaking. Do not stay silent", said Silence to Adam. This is the day that Silence screamed as loud as it ever has or ever could. Silence knew it had to speak to Adam.

Yet, today, Silence is still screaming. Perhaps, Silence is trying to get your attention and get you to cast it aside and speak up. It may be in the place you work or the church you attend. It could be that Silence has urged you to speak your mind to your neighbor, friend, relative, loved one or co-worker. "Speak", Silence is saying as you begin to walk away with the words yet in you. "Your remarks or advice could change the course of a disastrous outcome, but, if you keep Silence, your advice has no way to help anyone". Then Silence hears your excuse as you remark back to Silence, "They don't care what I have to say. After all, it doesn't matter because they would never listen to me any way". Silence turns to you in sternness and sincerity and remarks back, "How can they listen to you if you don't speak. Stop turning upon yourself in order to protect yourself. Help someone stay away from the path they can't see may harm them".

"Speak man, Speak woman, and tell your children you love them". "Speak from Silence and let your voice be heard, it does matter. If people will not or do not listen, at least you have come to the point where you are more concerned about protecting someone else instead of protecting yourself. In this process, you have grown. Your speaking up has helped you to discover something about your Silence. That is, Silence is not as golden at times, as some may want you to think. You have taken the step to let others know that you care about them enough, that you are willing to cast off Silence, and speak. You are willing to take steps to protect someone else instead of protecting the image you wish to project by keeping Silence as your best friend.

My friend, speak the truth in love. Speak with carefully chosen words. Speak when you know in your heart of hearts that you should. Make the ultimate concern to be the welfare of others. Stop hiding. The more you hide with your friend Silence, the harder it becomes to speak.

Now, it is time to decide. What will you do with Silence? Silence and Speech are to be servants and not masters. They are brothers with different personalities and concerns. Learn to use them both. Learn to make them your friends. Do not allow either to cause you to hide and protect yourself. Rather, use them both as servants that are willing to rush to the aid someone else. (Including yourself.)

Go ahead and catch yourself today. Be aware of the occasions when you know that you should speak up. Go ahead and tell Silence to sit down because you have something to say. Be equally aware, to know when you should make Silence your friend. Finally, ask God to help you know the difference.

What is it that you need to speak up about today? What thought have you been holding back because you are afraid? Do not turn around and walk away with the words in you when you know in your heart of hearts, that Silence is screaming for you to speak.

Too often as men, we follow the path of the first man, Adam. While the serpent was speaking to Eve, Adam kept silence. However, after Eve disobeyed God by partaking of the fruit, Adam was ready to speak up and blame Eve for the whole thing. Why is it that we are so ready to speak up and blame? Simply put, we are by our own lower nature, protecting ourselves from the responsibility of responsibility. Adam opened his mouth and blamed Eve when God approached him in the garden about what had happened.

Folks, let us learn something here. That is, speak up. You never know what difference you may make in the lives of people now and in the lives of people in the future.

We are still living with the decision that Adam made when he kept silent. Yet, do not be so hard on Adam. The fact remains, that we are doing the same thing in our day. Speak up and make a difference. Now.

When silence screamed-Write your thoughts

_____

_____

_____

_____

_____

_____

_____

_____

_____

_____

_____

_____

_____

_____

You Are Not Where You Are.
(But you could be)

This is an interesting thought to me. You are there, but then again, you are not there. You are where you are, but are you there? Let me explain.

How many times do we long to go somewhere (such as on vacation) and as soon as we get to our destination (if not sooner) we are not there? We long to be there until we get there, then we are not there. Instead, we began to go through the same routine as before. "Well, here we are, on the sandy beaches of the world. This is our vacation, a little get away from the same old thing." Perhaps, it is just for a weekend. Yet, it does not take long for the thoughts to flood your mind. "I wish I was at home, grandma's house, the lake, river, ocean, water puddle or somewhere else." Why do we always want to be where we are not? Why do we long for somewhere else besides where our feet are standing? Our heart seems to want to deny us the pleasure of having sand between our toes.

I really believe it would do us good to learn to "Be There." Where you are, be there. Live your life to the fullest wherever you may be. Relish the moment wherever you are and you will soon find that you will have a much more satisfying life ahead of you each day and each now.

Here is part of the problem. We have forgotten how to discover what is before us. We have been programmed to go at such a fast pace that we truly have not enjoyed even the most common things. We seem to have a knack of allowing the past and the future to kick the present moment around, or to cover it up and bury it. The past raises its voice to say, "Look at me" and you will be happy. Yet, the future trying to be louder than the past, screams out, "Oh no, look at me and you will be happier tomorrow, next week, or next year. In all of this, I ask, "Where is the present moment"? Where is now in all of this? It is there, but the past and the future are not willing to give up their position to now. Yet, if you will be rational and thoughtful, you will realize that all you really have is now. The past is just that, a span of time and events that has gone by. The future as we call it can never really be. Why, because when you arrive in the "future" it will be now. It is the same with later. There really is no later. There is only a future and a later as elements of a clock or calendar. Simply put, your perceived later is really now. I guess what I am trying to say is, what is so wrong with living now? You can never actually live in the future or later. You can only live and be now. You may plan your calendar for future events, but you cannot live that event until you arrive at the now of the event.

When was the last time that you really took a good long whiff of bacon and eggs frying while the coffee was on to brew? When was the last time you picked up one of the children, or your pet, looked into their eyes, and really noticed the color of them and the twinkle as they looked back at you? Have you taken the time to relish being able to see a cloud dance by your doorstep? What about the beautiful flowers? Sure, they look nice from afar off, but why not take the time to count the pedals and smell their fragrance? Learn to discover again. Learn to be where you are and really be there in the present moment. Come awake to yourself and your surroundings.

Remember how it was as a child. We would take the time to lie down in the grass and watch the clouds go by as we looked for a shape in them. We knew then how to discover and relish where we were and what we were doing. At that point, in our lives we were able to "Be There", in the present moment. We were able to forget about clock time, daytime, nighttime and yes, bed time.

Now, as adults, we want to be somewhere else, doing something else, with someone else, until we get to somewhere else, doing nothing else, with someone else. We seem to want to do what we are not doing. I think it strange, at least when you think of the truth that it was totally the opposite just a few years ago.

Do yourself a favor. Right now, stop reading and just take the time to look around you. What do you see that you have not seen before? Be there, in the moment. It is all you really have so relish that moment. Go out, count the pedals on some flower, and take time to smell its fragrance. Pick up your child and really notice the color of the eyes. Notice the ears, cheeks, nose, and mouth and discover what you have not seen before. Wiggle your toes, check your belly button for fuzz, listen to a bird sing or listen to yourself breath. Be awake and aware of what is around you and within you now. Be where you are now, in the present moment. Be There. Now.

Notice the different colors in the room. See which colors are lighter in nature and which are darker. What is in the present time and place that stands out and calls for your attention? Be there in the moment and see what you have been missing. Are you sitting next to a window? Look out, count the colors, and see them again for the first time.

Perhaps you could again really begin to enjoy being with others in the present moment. Give no thought as to how you may feel they perceive you to be. You just learn to allow yourself to be there with them in the moment and relish the time you have together. Do not work at trying to impress them. Rather, just allow yourself, to be you. Do not work at trying to gather up a crumb of approval from your friends, relatives, co-workers, church members or anyone else. Instead, just be you and relish the time together. Have such a good time with life that others will be glad that you are a part of their now.

Wherever you are, be there. It is time you enjoyed life more, in the moment.

Go ahead, right now and do it. Be in the moment.

Relish the moment. Make the most of the moment you have. In fact, you cannot really "have" the past. Neither can you really grasp the future. All you really have is the moment. Live it like it will never be there again, because it will not be. You cannot live in the past neither can there ever be a future. All we have is the moment at any time of life.

It is sort of like saying that there never really is such thing as later. This is because that once you get to the time line of later; it is really the present moment. Therefore, because you cannot live later, you must live now.

Remember, Relish the moment, now, it is the only now your have.

You are not where you are-Write your thoughts

_____

_____

_____

_____

_____

_____

_____

Thank You

I want to express my appreciation to you for choosing to read this book. Your time is valuable and you have used a chunk of it reading this book. It is time that you will never be able to get back. It is my sincere desire that this book has helped you and that you believe it was good use of your time to read it.

There is another book in the making already. Watch for it sometime in mid 2005.

If you have any questions, comments or concerns, please feel free to write me.

Email address: bgerding@sbcglobal.net

Drop me a line in the mail. My address is:

Dr. Bob Gerding

P.O. Box 282

Boonville, Mo. 65233

Again, thank you and have a greater day.

Sincerely,

Dr. Bob Gerding

About the Author

The author brings you this book because he has a love for writing and helping others to excel. As a part time computer instructor, he understands the fears and uncertainties of those in class. These fears and uncertainties go beyond the classroom into everday life. It is the desire of the author to help us to see ourselves in a different but truthful way. Each chapter was written with you in mind. The truth is, you are not that much different from anyone else, including the author. You will no doubt see yourself in this book.

19546790R00060

Made in the USA
Lexington, KY
24 December 2012